Rose Windows and how to make them

Helga Meyerbröker

Rose Windows and how to make them

Coloured tissue paper crafts

Floris Books

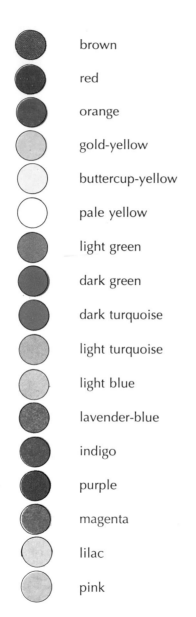

brown

red

orange

gold-yellow

buttercup-yellow

pale yellow

light green

dark green

dark turquoise

light turquoise

light blue

lavender-blue

indigo

purple

magenta

lilac

pink

Translated by Polly Lawson

Photographs by Birgitt Gutermuth

First published in German under the title
Transparente Bilder und Rosetten aus Seidenpapier
by Frech Verlag in 1989
First published in English in 1994 by Floris Books
Third impression 1995

British Library CIP Data available

ISBN 0-86315-196-5

Printed in Belgium

Contents

Figure 2.

The basic technique

Material and equipment

Large ready-made card ringswith outside diameter about 11" (28 cm), inside diameter
about 9" (23 cm)
Small card rings with outside diameter about
7" (18 cm), inside diameter about 5¾"
(14.5 cm)
Coloured tissue paper
Non-drip adhesive (avoid liquid adhesive)
Pencil
Scissors (fine handwork scissors, or slightly
curved nail-scissors)

If you cannot buy card rings you can cut them
out yourself from photographic card using a
pair of compasses and the measurements indicated. In this case you can choose a frame to
suit the colours. But remember: against the
light you will hardly notice the colour of the
frame, and a neutral colour such as grey or
beige is quite sufficient for all the tissue paper
combinations.

Folding techniques

The first examples are very simple to do, but
they open the way for a great number of variations.
    What appears a bit long and tedious in the
description hardly takes any time after you
have done it once. So take heart!

1. First take two small card rings (7", 18 cm
diameter).

2. Select following colours of tissue paper:
    Foundation — white
    First layer — light turquoise
    Second layer — lime-green
    Third layer — dark turquoise
    Fourth layer — lavender-blue.

Figure 3. Fold in half.

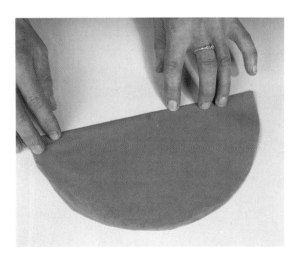

9

Lay the sheets one on top of the other with the white on top. Mark the circumference of the inside of the ring with a pencil. Cut out all the sheets together with a seam allowance of about ¼" (0.5–1 cm). This allowance will disappear later under the second framing ring and so does not need to be cut out very neatly.

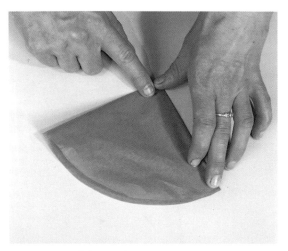

Figure 4. Fold into four.

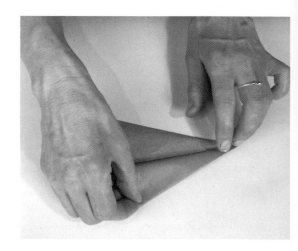

Figure 6. Fold into sixteen.

Figure 5. Fold into eight.

Figure 7.

3. Glue the white sheet onto the inner card ring (using the pencilled circle as a guide to make it fit). The white sheet now serves as the foundation for the next layer.

4. Now the remaining four cut-out sheets must be folded in the same way:

Fold in half (Figure 3)

Fold in half again (Figure 4)

Fold in half again (Figure 5), holding together the edges which want to spring apart.

Fold in half again (to a sixteenth of the original size) but this time fold half of the bundle upwards and flip the other half downwards (Figure 6).

It is important to be very precise with these folds, with the creases running to an exact point and the sides pressed down flat. The symmetry of the finished article depends on precision at this stage (Figure 7).

From now on these folded pieces will be called *wedges*.

5. Lay the four wedges beside each other so that they make quarter of a circle with the lightest colour (first layer) on the left, then the

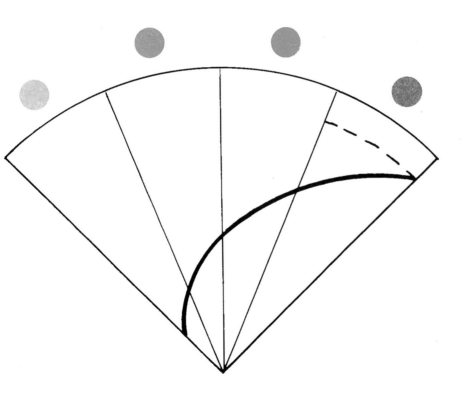

Figure 8.

Figure 9.

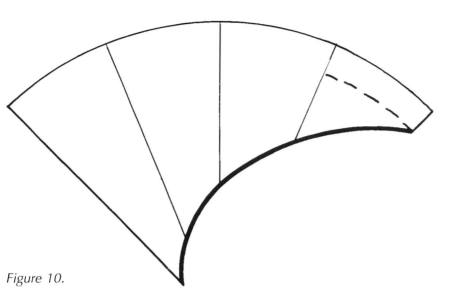

Figure 10.

second layer and the third; and finally the darkest on the right. Mark the seam allowance on this wedge (Figure 8).

6. Mark the heavy curved line in Figure 8 onto the wedges which you have in front of you. Cut along this line on each wedge. Lay the four cut-off points of the wedges to one side for later use. You now have all the sections as shown in Figures 9 and 10.

7. Unfold the lightest-coloured and longest cut-out wedge, smoothing out the creases as you unfold (this can be done with your finger-nail).

8. Now lay the pieces onto the base, covering the white foundation evenly. Glue them on in the same way as the white tissue paper was glued onto the card ring (Figure 9).

9. Unfold the second part and smooth it out. Now take care: *all* the creases made while folding must lie *exactly* on top of each other. It does not matter whether the crease is facing up or down (mountain or valley), but what is important is that the creases which belong to the pattern lie on top of each other. In the present example the arches overlap, so that all the cut lines round about appear to run parallel. Once the second layer is correctly positioned it can be glued in place.

Do the same with the third wedge and then with the fourth.

14

Achieving the correct alignment of the creases is a matter of practice. If you find this difficult at the beginning, the following may be helpful.

First align the vertical creases in the direction of the arrows (see Figure 15). Then push them up or down until the remaining creases coincide.

In this way all the creases will lie correctly.

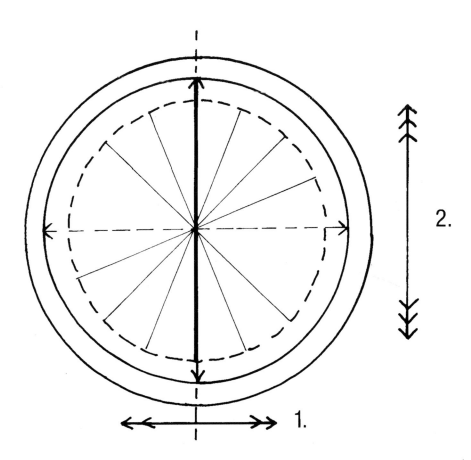

Figure 12.

Figure 13.

10. The second card ring should now cover the ugly glue area and reinforce the frame at the same time, so make sure that it is well glued!

11. To finish off, pass a thread through the frame so that it can be hung up. Hold the whole thing up against the light and experiment with which way it hangs most effectively in order to find where best to make the hole for the thread (see Figure 11).

12. The cut-off wedge points can be used in various decorative ways. Unfold the points, smooth them out and glue them together, one on top of the other according to size (it is enough to put a spot of glue in the middle). You can use these flowerlike stars for decoration, when for example wrapping gifts (Figure 13).

Variation on the basic

If you use the same colours for this variation as those used in the first example, you will be able to compare the two examples for effect; but you can also try out a new colour combination (Figure 15). For example,
   light blue
   lavender-blue
   lavender-blue again
   and magenta.

Repeat stages 1 to 8 as described on pages 9–13.

9. Unfold and smooth out the second wedge, but now glue it in a different way: do not lay the arches on top of each other, but displace them by a crease (Figure 14).
   Continue steps 10 and 11 as described on page 7.

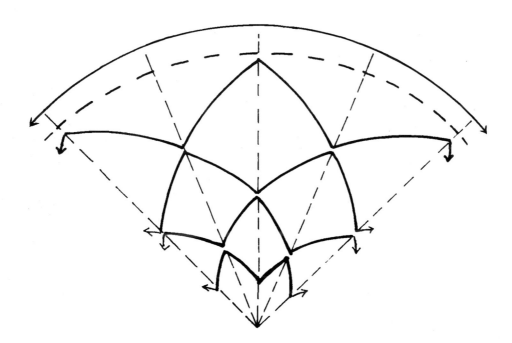

Figure 14.

Figure 15.

Further variations

From this simple basis all kinds of variations can be developed. The significant factor is the way in which the lines cutting *all* four wedges are drawn.

Some possibilities are explained in Figures 17-19.

Figure 16.

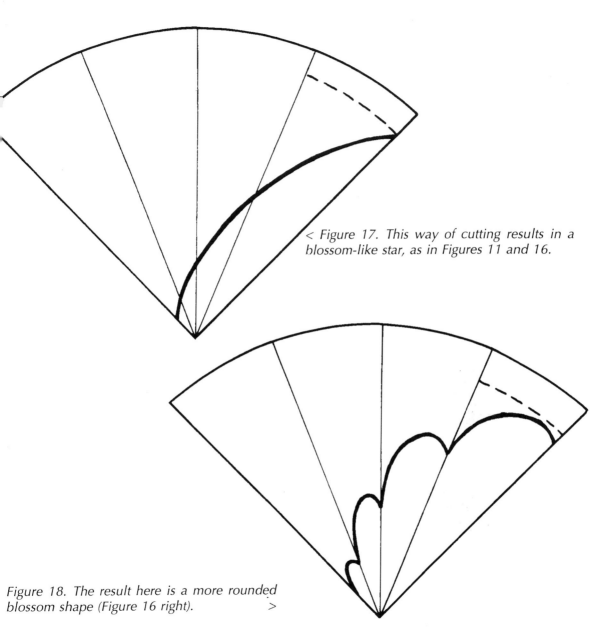

< Figure 17. This way of cutting results in a blossom-like star, as in Figures 11 and 16.

Figure 18. The result here is a more rounded blossom shape (Figure 16 right).   >

21

This indicates some of the potential variety. We should mention however that each way of cutting can produce two patterns if you take into account the displacement of the arches. It is also worth trying out the same pattern in two different colour combinations, radiant yellow tones for example will produce an effect quite different from that made by deep luminous blue.

Figure 19. The result of this serrated cut produces the lovely effect of gossamer as in Figure 20.

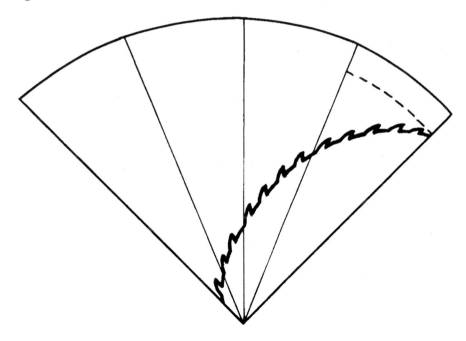

Figure 20.

23

Figure 21.

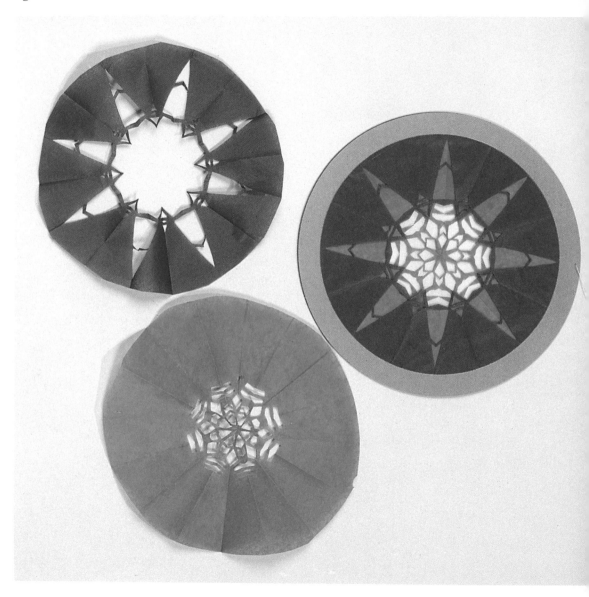

Stars

A small star

With the next patterns a new process is added, namely the cutting out of the patterns. This is almost always done by cutting into the sides of the wedges, as will be seen in the diagrams accompanying each star (Figures 22, 23, 26 and 29).

We begin with a simple star consisting of only two colours (plus the white background).

The *lighter* colour, in this case light turquoise, is used for cutting out the pattern — and in this way we obtain the beautiful openwork centre.

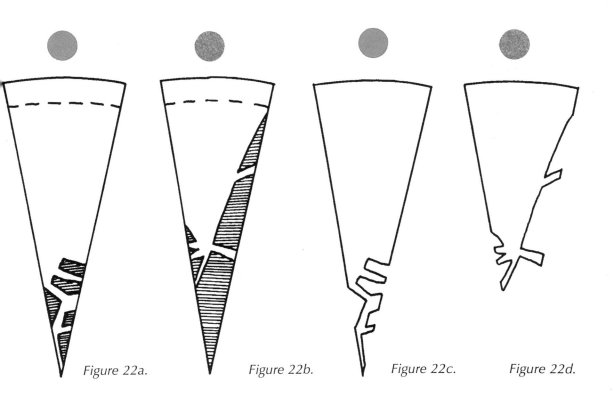

Figure 22a.   Figure 22b.   Figure 22c.   Figure 22d.

The second *stronger* colour, lavender-blue produces the outer star shape (Figure 21). With these two colours, light turquoise and lavender-blue, we can apply stages 1 to 4 of pages 10–11.

5. Copy the hatched pattern of Figure 22a onto the light-coloured wedge, then with a fine pair of scissors cut out the hatched part (beginning at the side), taking care not to accidently cut through the arms. You will be left with the shape in Figure 22c.
Copy Figure 22b to the dark-coloured wedge and cut out accordingly (Figure 22d).

6. Unfold both wedges fold by fold and smooth out. Take care with the delicate points!

7. First glue the lighter colour (light turquoise) onto the white background. Lay the darker colour (lavender-blue) on top. Crease, align and stick it at the edge.

8. Cover with the second ring of card and finish off by hanging it from a thread.

Variation of the small star

This variation enables us to cut out a sixteen-point star from the same folding as the eight-pointed star.
Use the colours orange and a strong red. Follow the same procedure as for the first star, but at step 5 copy Figure 23a onto the orange wedge and Figure 23b to the red.
The finished sixteen-point star is shown in Figure 24.

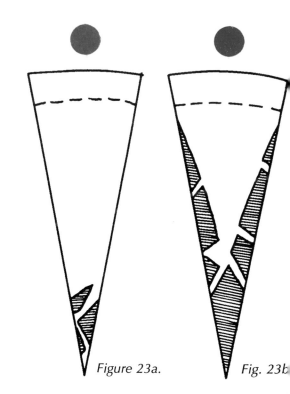

Figure 23a.　　　　Fig. 23b

This principle of allowing the pattern to become visible or to shine through a further layer forms the basis for the next designs.

And of course the larger the diameter the more scope for creativity. For this reason we shall use the larger card rings (11", 28 cm diameter, see page 9) in the next examples.

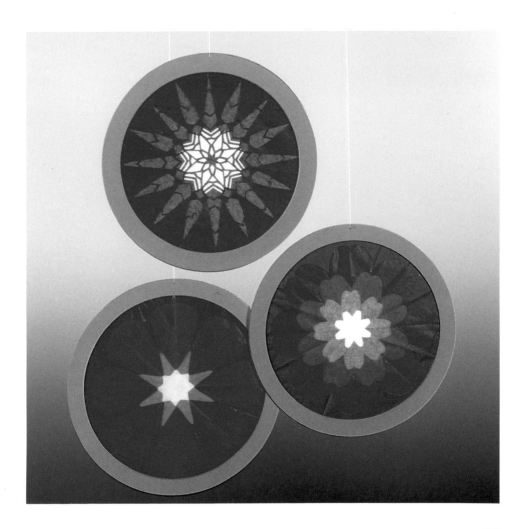

Figure 24.

Large star

For this very clearly structured star a third colour is added.

You will need two large rings (11", 28 cm diameter), tissue paper in light blue, lavender-blue, indigo, and the usual white for the foundation.

By now you will probably be quite familiar with each stage of the work (but if not, refer back to the *small star* on page 25). This time fold the three colours, copy the corresponding three cutting-out patterns onto the wedges and cut them out (see Figure 26).

Figure 25 shows the finished star (left) and the three stages leading up to it. You will see how the light blue is positioned to create the light effect in the middle, the lavender-blue helps to form the whole star and the indigo gives the whole design its distinct form and definite outlines.

Figure 25.

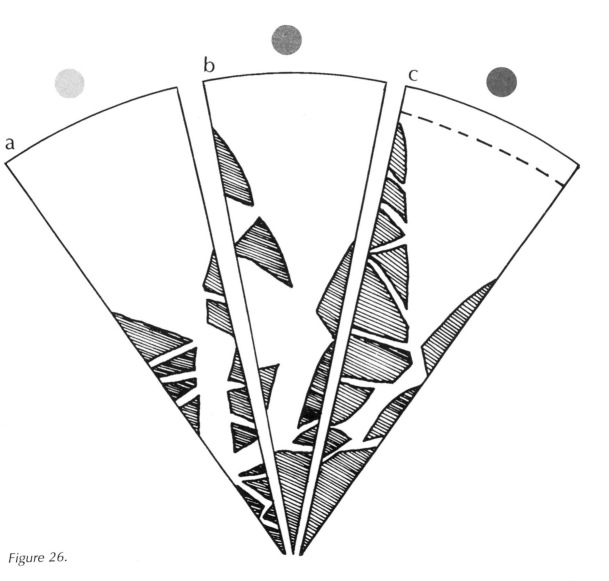

Figure 26.

Figure 27.

Yellow star

The yellow star in Figure 28 is very simple to cut out although it looks quite complicated at first sight. It has an almost three-dimensional effect. This is because it is cut out in the shape of a star, becoming larger and broader as it moves from light to dark. This effect is increased by adding two extra layers of colour.

For this model four colours are required apart from the white foundation:

pale yellow
buttercup-yellow (twice)
gold yellow.

Copy the cutting-out pattern for each colour from Figure 29a–e.

Figure 28.

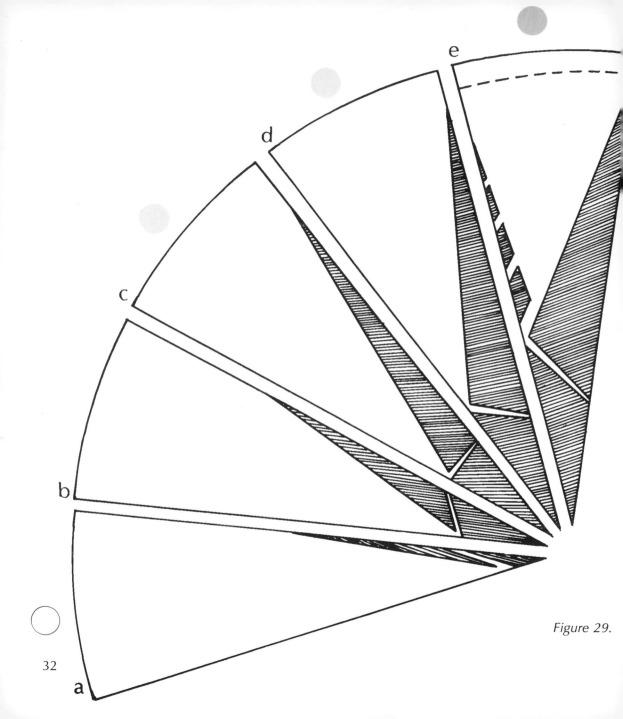

a
b
c
d
e

32

Figure 29.

Snow star

The snow crystal in Figure 32 is a six-pointed star. This basic structure leads directly to the crystal, but you need to follow a slightly different procedure for the folding:

Once you have folded the circle of paper in half and then in half again (in step 4 of page 10), you divide the resulting quarter into three segments. In this way you will arrive at a

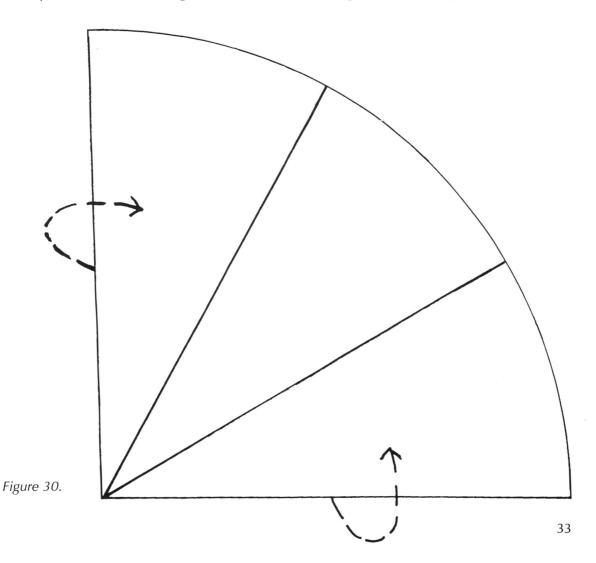

Figure 30.

wedge made up of twelve folds and it will be wider then the wedges you have worked with in previous designs (see Figure 30).

There are innumerable variations of snow crystals in nature. Here we only give a sketch of the shape of the crystal which is the basis of Figure 32.

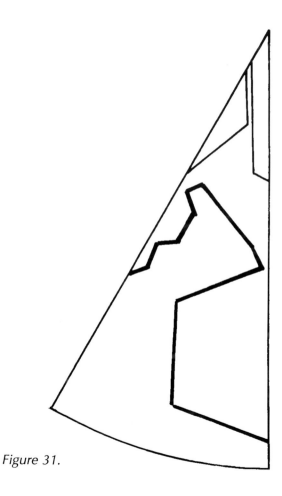

Figure 31.

Figure 32. >

Figure 34. >

Rosettes

The following three examples will enable you
to become familiar with the principle of how
rosettes are made.

All three consist of the same colours:
pink
lavender-blue
magenta.

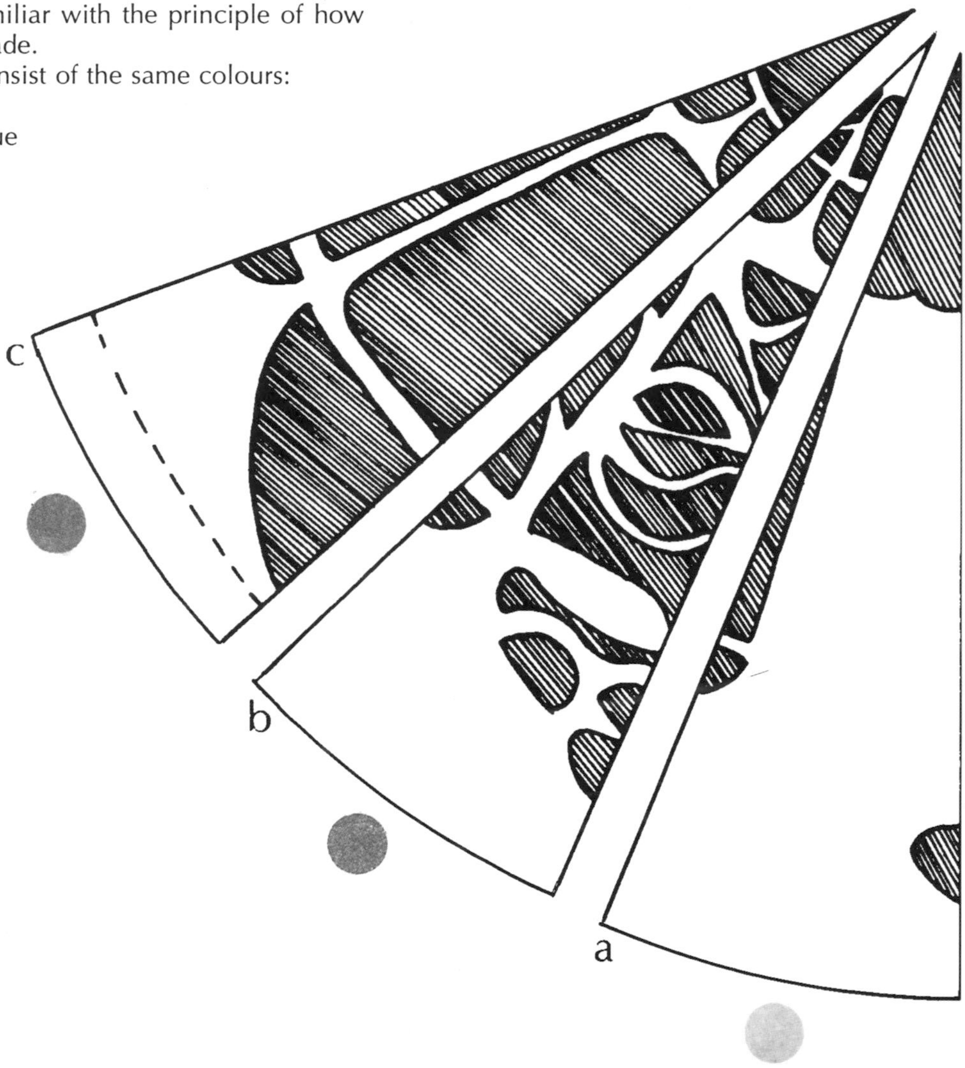

c

b

a

Figure 33.

36

The first example has a fairly simple pattern, so the basic principle is easily recognizable. The other models are more intricate, in increasingly complex variations of the basic pattern.

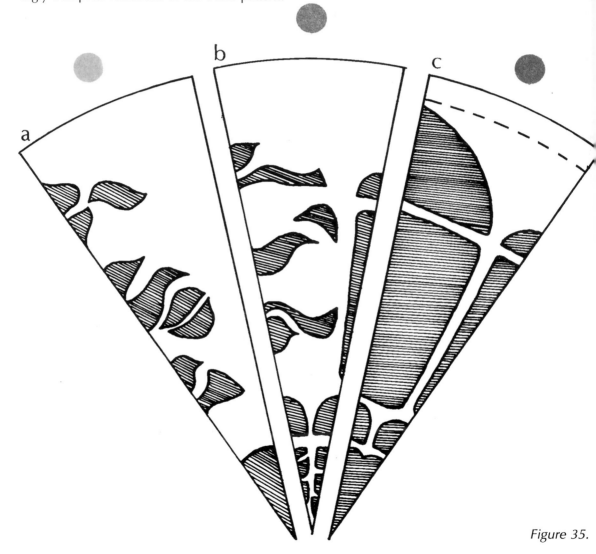

Figure 35.

Rosette 1

Let us begin with the rosette on the left in Figure 34. After folding copy the pattern of Figure 33 onto the wedges. Cut off the point of the pink wedge. This allows the open-work centre to become visible in the lavender-blue layer. Very little is cut out from rest of the pink (see Figure 33a).

The lavender-blue circle spreads out like filigree over the pink surface and has a rather more complicated pattern. Some of the hatched parts can no longer be cut out from the side, so you must insert the point of the scissors carefully into the wedge in order to make the start of the cut (Figure 33b).

Figure 36.

Figure 37.

40

The magenta circle shows up the rosette shape well and is cut away extensively (Figure 33c).

Figure 36 shows the three stages.

Rosette 2

For the second example (see Figure 33 bottom right) also fold:

pink
lavender-blue
magenta.

Copy the pattern in Figure 35a–c.

Pink and lavender-blue are placed so that the different colours show through the cuts alternately (Figures 35a and 35b).

Magenta is positioned in exactly the same way as in the first example, so that the rosette shape appears (Figure 35c).

Rosette 3

The third rosette can be seen in Figure 34 (top).

Fold the same colours. Copy Figure 38a–c onto the respective wedges.

The cutting-out patterns for pink and lavender-blue are almost identical to the second example, but magenta encloses all the cut-out surfaces and so produces the distinctive pattern of the whole rosette and the marked outlines.

These three examples of the rosette are developed on an eightfold pattern. You can develop a sixteenfold pattern for the rosettes (Figure 37) as was shown with the stars.

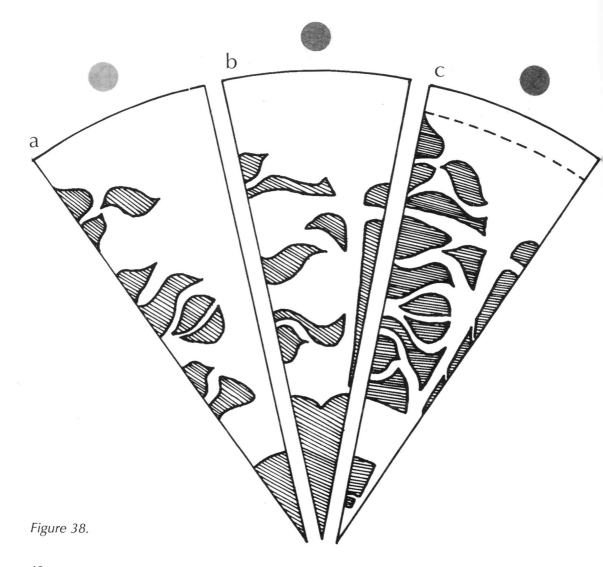

Figure 38.

Sixteenfold rosette

The sixteenfold rosette consists of four colours:
    dark turquoise
    lavender-blue
    dark green
    magenta.

Figure 39 shows each stage clearly:
    Dark turquoise appears mainly in the centre and releases a few points of light (Figure 40a).
    Lavender-blue (with turquoise beneath) fills in a 'window' eight times (Figure 40b).

Figure 39.

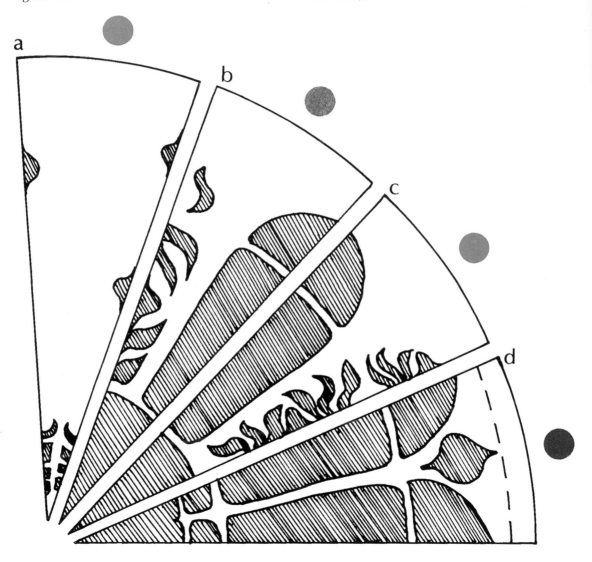

Figure 40.

Dark green (also with turquoise beneath) fills in the neighbouring windows (Figure 40c).

Magenta frames all sixteen windows (Figure 40d).

a

b

c

d

Gothic rose windows

The rosette of the Figure 42 takes its inspiration from a Gothic cathedral. It is also a sixteenfold rosette consisting of four colours:

    lavender-blue

    magenta

    red

    purple.

Figures 41a-d apply to this rosette, but note that these patterns are for a slightly smaller ring with outer diameter about 10½" (26 cm) and inner diameter about 8½" (21 cm).

Figure 41.

The peculiarity of Figure 43 is that apart from the small inner part it shows no pattern, but consists of coloured surfaces.

Figure 42.

Figure 43.

Figure 44.

Figure 44 has a distinctive flower pattern while Figure 45 shows motifs like folk-art. These two examples are shown to stimulate your own creativity.

Figure 45.

Tips

With practice you will acquire your own expertise. We will, however, add a few hints here.

The *colours* suggested in the particular examples are combinations which have been tried out frequently, but if you have not got a specific colour in stock you will be able to manage with another which is as close as possible to the missing one. Or you can try out your own ideas. As a caution however, it is advisable to keep to the pattern of moving from light to dark, and to hold up the whole selection to the light before you begin, to test whether there is enough transparency. Reliable choices can only be made when testing against the light, rather than when light simply falls on the colours.

The preference for *white* as a foundation gives all the other colours an equal chance of attaining the optimal brilliance. A light blue foundation for example, may help further shades of blue to a greater intensity, but other colours will be distorted. It should not be forgotten that white lets through the most light and gives the richest contrast.

Achieving the *open-work* of the luminescent *centre-pieces* is not necessarily a matter of cutting out as many and as tiny pieces as possible. The finer the remaining webs are, the more likely the centre is to attain that attractive filigree character.

Tissue paper unfortunately is not *resistant to fading,* so as far as possible, it should not be subjected to direct sunlight. If you can avoid direct sunlight the sheets will last longer, so it is a good idea to put them on north and east facing windows. The colours fade at different rates. Yellow proves surprisingly light-resistant, but pink colours often fade fairly quickly.

Damp is also a danger: direct drops of water leave distinct holes in the colour, so watch out for condensation on the window panes. Variations in humidity and room temperature mean that warping is unavoidable.

Paper, after all, is for short-lived works of art, so we should perhaps accept deterioration simply as an incentive for fresh creation.

Making transparencies

Pictures made with tissue paper, which we shall simply call transparencies, come alive when light shines through them. When it is viewed only in the light falling directly onto it, its effect is often disappointing, as the top layer of intensive colour obscures the interesting composition below.

The full interplay of the colours is masked in direct light, but is revealed when the light shines through the picture. The particular character of the colours, quite independent of the quality of the composition, is revealed only in the changing light of day. As the day breaks only a small amount of light streams through the picture, gently tinging the colours, which come to their full strength later in the day. Towards evening, in the fading light, they appear quite different again. This changing interplay of light and colour gives us a heightened pleasure.

Method

In the first part the method of folding described is ornamental in character because the patterns are made up of symmetrical repetitions of a single design, always enclosed in a round frame. This technique remains to a certain extent limited, even though there are no bounds to the scope for creativity because of the incredible number of possible colour combinations and designs.

In this second part a completely different method is described which can remind us of the veils in water-colour painting, in which the colours are laid on top of each other producing new colour-variations and new lines.

This greater freedom of design opens up new possibilities, and creative activity can develop in fresh directions.

Characteristics of tissue paper

While in the first part of the book the tissue paper was cut, it is now also torn.

All tissue paper has a *grain* (or tear-direction). You can make a fairly straight tear along this grain. If you tear slowly and bear down upon the paper with your other hand you can create deliberate curves and arcs. If you tear against the grain you may find that the paper unexpectedly crumples or comes away in ragged edges. Both directions of tearing can be used for particular purposes so it is worth experimenting at the edge first.

Cutting the paper gives a very smooth edge which shows up more sharply than the softer edge made by tearing. For special effects a motif can be cut out from a prepared background (through several layers), for example whenever something has to be brought into relief.

For the following fairy-tale motif all three methods will be used: tearing, cutting, and the cutting-in process of the first method.

gure 46.

Figure 47.

Star-money —
A fairy-tale scene

Materials and equipment

Cardboard for the frames
Whole pieces of tissue paper:
   white
   light blue
   light turquoise
   dark turquoise
   light blue
   lavender-blue
   indigo
   brown
   magenta
Offcuts in following colours:
   pink or brown for face, hands and legs
   pale yellow for the dress
   gold-yellow, brown or black for the hair
Adhesive
Pencil
Cling-film and paper-clips
Fine and medium-blade scissors
Ruler or rectangular triangle
Knife for cutting cardboard

Note:
The patterns in Figures 48, 49, 50, 52
and 55 are reduced to 75% of true size.

Figure 48.

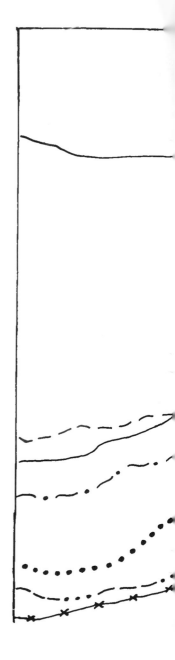

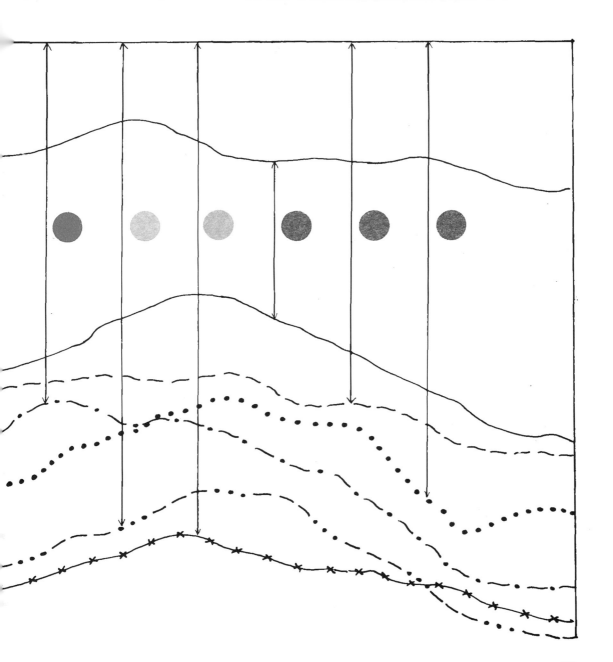

55

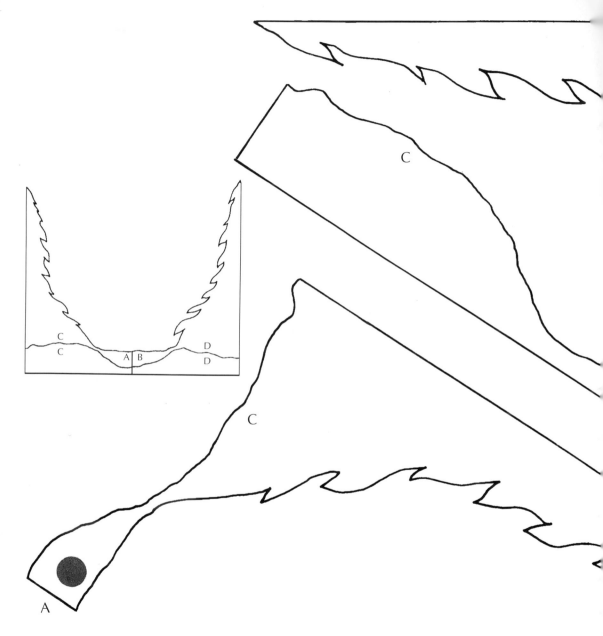

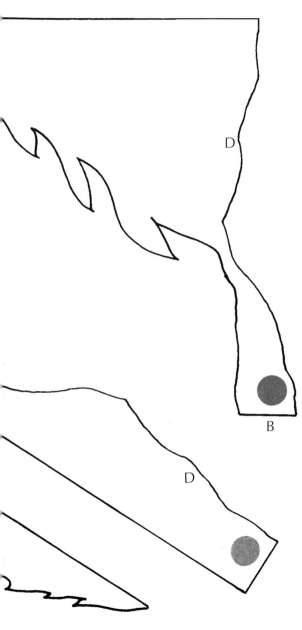

The background

Begin with two layers of light blue about 14½" (37 cm) long and 11½" (29 cm) wide.

Stick these together at the edges to make the foundation for the picture. (For a lighter-coloured motif use a white foundation).

The sky

For the sky you will need six sheets to start with:

light turquoise
dark turquoise
light blue
three sheets of lavender-blue.

Lay these six colours on top of each other and cut them to size 11½" x 9" (29 x 23 cm).

Figure 48 shows you how to tear the lower arc (the arc is 11½", 29 cm wide, the height varies). The patterns are reduced to 75% of true size. That means they must be enlarged to 133%.

Note that the lowest lavender-blue strip also has an arc torn upwards, so that the picture in the upper part will not be too dark.

Glue the following in order along the edge of the sides (see Figure 46):

light turquoise
light blue
lavender-blue 1
lavender-blue 2
lavender-blue 3

Figure 49.

Light blue and light turquoise peep out from below, while the topmost lavender-blue layer covers the three middle layers and so softens the tear-lines (Figure 47).

Now turn the whole thing over and lay the dark background for the trees on the back. For this take brown tissue paper, size 11½" x 11" (29 x 28 cm). Cut according to Figure 49. Tear an indigo strip about 2" (5 cm) wide, as shown in the same Figure 49.

First glue brown then indigo to the sides, as shown in Figure 52.

Trees

Now come the trees. The colours are chosen to produce a mood of darkness, so there are no warm or even green shades, but there are a few lighter colours for the brighter part in the middle:

    two layers of magenta
    two layers indigo
    three layers of dark turquoise
    two layers of light blue
    two layers of brown
    one layer of light turquoise.
Size about 8½" x 6" (22 x 15 cm)

Copy the trees from Figures 50a and 50b. It is not important to make an exact copy, but the size and shape of the branches should roughly correspond. It is advisable to clip the layers together with paper-clips before cutting out to prevent them slipping. This will enable you to cut out all twelve layers in one operation.

Figure 50a.

Figure 50b.

Figure 51.

Now you will have twelve large trees and twelve smaller ones. By staggering these in layers you cán make a realistic 'forest' which at first glance hides the fact that it has been built up from only one tree-form in two sizes, and looks quite natural. This effect is produced not only by the different colours but also by the asymmetrical shape of the trees. To enhance this effect it is a good idea to turn some of the trees round and stick them the other way round, thus breaking the uniformity of the forest.

Glue the larger, darker trees towards the edge (sticking them down by their tops and the base of their trunks) and glue the smaller, lighter ones towards the middle.

From the store of trees the following are large ones are used:

one magenta
two indigo
two dark turquoise
two light blue

and following small ones:

one magenta
one indigo
two brown
three dark turquoise
two light blue
and one light turquoise.

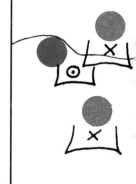

Figure 52.

to the left 9 trees

✕   4 big ones

☉   5 small ones

to the right 8 trees

✕   4 big ones

☉   4 small ones

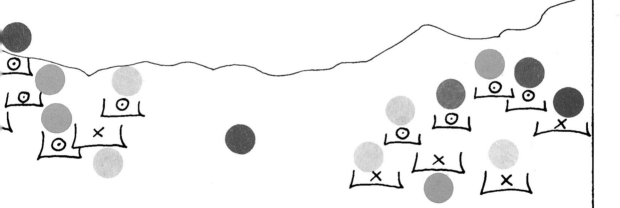

Figure 53.

Figure 54 shows the approximate arrangement of the trees, Figure 52 shows the arrangement more accurately.

Vary the level on which the trees stand, with some higher and others lower. A brown strip (Figure 52) covers the varying levels.

Figure 54.

The stars

Next cut out of stars. For this you will need a fine pair of scissors with points that cut well.

You may wish to practise cutting out a star beforehand, but the stars will look more natural if their shape is slightly irregular. There should be not more than twenty, and it is good to have one or two larger ones. A few should be clearly visible on the open dress, and those in the sky should be arranged into little constellations rather then evenly. Finally you can add a few extra little stars by cutting into the paper with your fine scissors.

You will now have done the most laborious part.

The girl

Now copy the figure of the girl from Figure 55, remembering that the pattern is reduced to 75% of the final size. Place it well into the middle of a piece of white tissue paper about 11½" x 7" (29 x 18 cm).

Now place the figure onto the prepared picture so that she stands amongst the trees with her feet resting on the brown strip. Make sure that the girl stands absolutely vertically, so that she does not look as if she is about to fall forwards or backwards. Once you have got her in the right position secure the white paper to the sides with adhesive tape (you can also add a bit of glue in the middle of her dress).

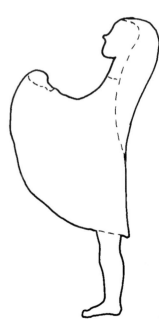

Figure 55.

With your fine scissors cut along the outlines through all the layers. Some ends of branches which are in the way will fall off at the same time. Cut the outline of the face carefully be- cause a small slip might give the poor child a grotesque nose, for example.

The pattern can then be dispensed with. Turn the whole thing over, glue a sheet of

Figure 56.

white tissue paper to the back to cover the whole area and cut off any protruding edges.

The figure is still snow-white from head to foot. For the parts which are skin-coloured use a light pink or brown. Copy the lower legs, the hands and the face onto a double piece of pink tissue paper from Figure 55. Cut them slightly larger so that no white shows through any-

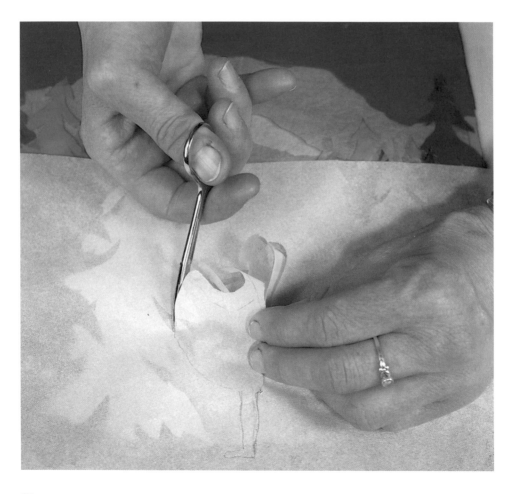

Figure 57.

where. Glue the face on single-fold, the hands double but staggered a bit, and the legs likewise. (The pink may appear rather bright but will soon fade.)

The gown consists firstly of a little piece of pale yellow tissue paper about 3½" x 3½" (9 x 9 cm). Crumple it on one side so that it fits at the neck-opening and appears pleated (Figure

Figure 58.

59). Lay this piece to one side for a moment. Now apply plenty of glue to the place where the gown is to come (Figure 58). Lay the 'dress' onto the glue surface and work it into the right gown shape. Indicate the position of the arms by making folds accordingly (Figure 59).

By using plenty of glue you will have enough time to work the dress into a gown

Figure 59.

Figure 60.

before the glue sets. This is also a question of practice, but you can soon achieve mastery in the art of making folds. Now cut off what is left over with your scissors (Figure 59 again).

If you enjoy this crinkle-technique you can also make the hair in this way. Use a generous piece of gold-yellow, brown or black. We recommend that you glue on an identical piece to cover it, which will also strengthen the colour. The alternative is to cut out two or three 'hair-does' as in Figure 55 and stick them on flat. You do not need to work on the details of the face — this usually only spoils it.

The frame

Now all that is lacking is the enclosing frame which needs to cover the ugly gluey patches at the edges and give the picture the necessary stability for hanging up. If you've never made a card frame for a picture before, don't worry; it isn't difficult. I have worked from a model with inside measurements of 14" (35 cm) high and 11" (27 cm) wide, but during the work some displacement sometimes occurs or a stray glue spot needs to be hidden beneath the frame. So check the inside measurements by attaching the picture to the window with cling-film and working out the best proportions.

The framing is a highly individual affair. If you have your own particular ideas and feel confident, you can follow your own taste, starting with the choice of colour for the frame.

I have chosen a neutral frame in white with a frame-width of 1½" (3.5 cm) (Figure 60). You may of course wish to choose a narrower frame but remember that it will not have as much stability. For the inside measurements of 14" x 11" (35 x 27 cm) the outside measurements will be 16½" x 13½" (42 x 34 cm).

Mark the outside measurements on the inner side of the cardboard which has not got the layers, and draw the outer edge of the frame with a pencil. Now mark in the width of the frame 1½" (3.5 cm) on each side and draw the inner edge. Cut out the two parts of the frame at the same time with a very sharp knife. Lay the two 'boards' together with the layered sides back to back and secure them with paper-clips to prevent them slipping. Cutting out both boards at the same time requires some strength, alternatively you can cut out each board separately.

Lay one part of the frame down with the inside facing up. Now lay the picture onto it so that the glued edges lie evenly on the frame, and make sure that the trees and the figure are standing vertically. Seal everything together with cling-film and lay it against the window to see how it looks. Once you have the motif sitting well in the frame apply glue to the frame and to the edge of the paper. Lay the second covering-frame onto it and press down firmly. Leave the whole thing under pressure for one to two hours because if the picture is hung up when the glue has not set properly, the frame may warp. Now all that is needed are two holes (about 3¼", 8 cm from the side) and a thread to hang the picture up.

Lantern children

This motif, uses darkness effectively and allows children's lanterns to shine against the light in a way that is hardly possible with a painting technique. This is the particular attraction of this motif (Figure 61).

Here are a few practical hints. First the background should be made of different blue or brown shades, plus a narrow strip of green for the horizon. The dark trees are torn out roughly and shaped by using the crinkling method. Unlike in the *Star-money* picture the figures are not cut out from the background but are added to it. For this the silhouettes are cut out in relatively dark colours and glued on in two layers. The face is simply cut from one of the layers. In this way it is gently indicated, and shows up as being lighter than its surroundings. Cut out the lanterns through all the layers. A white back-sheet added afterwards provides the surface for gluing on the coloured Chinese lanterns. Do not forget the lantern-sticks and a few stars in the dark sky.

Many other motifs are possible: such as specific motifs with great detail (and here a good pair of scissors is vital for exact work) or freely-drawn landscapes (Figure 62) which may be created most successfully by tearing rather than cutting, or abstract colour and shape studies (Figure 63).

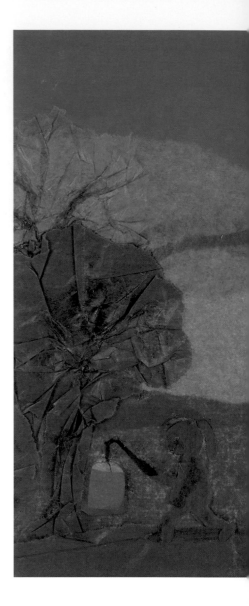

Figure 61.

Figure 62.

Figure 63.

r this type of work we recommend a
x-surface lit from below which enables you
see each stage (a glass pane with a light
low is enough to begin with).

Painted Japan-paper can be used for this
example. This cloth-like and expensive material
is obtainable only in a small range of colour
and has not quite the same brilliance as tissue
paper. But it is worth working with because of
its interesting composition and its resistance to
fading.